An Entrepreneur's Playbook

10 Power Plays for Business Success

Ora M. Chisom, MBA, PMP

AN ENTREPRENEUR'S PLAYBOOK

Dedication

This book is dedicated to you—the aspiring entrepreneurs, the dreamers who dare to envision a better future, the doers in their relentless pursuit of success, and all who harbor the ambition to create, innovate, and lead in the vast world of business. Here's to turning visions into ventures, transforming challenges into opportunities, and making dreams reality.

.

Table of Contents

Introduction

Ready to dive into the exhilarating world of entrepreneurship? Brace yourself for a rollercoaster ride of epic proportions where innovation meets opportunity, and bold ideas transform into thriving enterprises.

Entrepreneurship is more than just launching a business; it's a mindset and a lifestyle. Despite the obstacles, entrepreneurs' resilience, adaptability, and relentless pursuit of knowledge significantly boost their odds of success.

Driven by vision, they are always on the lookout for innovative solutions to disrupt conventional industries. What distinguishes them is their skill in overcoming challenges and turning failures into valuable learning experiences.

When I first leaped into entrepreneurship as a solopreneur, grand ideas of becoming a business owner didn't motivate me. Sheer necessity did. After leaving school and entering the workforce, let's just say my take-home pay wasn't quite enough to take me home. Leveraging my business and computer science background, I freelanced to supplement my income.

Through years of navigating the unpredictable waters of entrepreneurship, I've learned valuable lessons amidst the twists and turns of this adventurous journey. I admit, it hasn't been all smooth sailing on the business seas. The journey has included more twists, turns, and unexpected detours than a GPS with a sense of humor.

But fear not, readers! This book is a guiding compass on the path to entrepreneurial success, offering practical insights and addressing the unique challenges in an engaging manner. In "An Entrepreneur's Playbook: 10 Power Plays for Business Success," you'll discover the secrets of thriving entrepreneurs and learn how to turn daunting tasks into achievable goals. Whether you're looking to escape the 9-to-5 grind or achieve financial freedom, this book is designed to equip you with the tools needed to start, manage, and grow a business you can truly be proud of!

Play #1: Master an Entrepreneurial Mindset

Think of yourself as on the threshold of unparallel success. A whole, clear, glorious life lies before you. Achieve! Achieve! – Andrew Carnegie

In the fast-paced and ever-changing world of small business entrepreneurship, developing and maintaining the right mindset is crucial to achieving success. The entrepreneur mindset encompasses a unique set of attitudes, beliefs, and behaviors that separates successful entrepreneurs from the rest. It is characterized by a relentless pursuit of growth, a willingness to embrace uncertainty, and a strong belief in one's ability to create impact.

To be successful, you must turn off negative self-talk and limiting beliefs, strap on some faith and confidence, pour yourself a cup of ambition, and get your head in the game.

Overcoming Limiting Beliefs

Have you heard the terms "limiting beliefs" or "fixed mindset" before? They mean the same thing and quite simply, these are beliefs, often established in early childhood which can become major stumbling blocks when trying to create a profitable, successful business.

Everyone brings a unique set of experiences shaped by their diverse backgrounds, cultures, and identities to the entrepreneurial table. These diverse perspectives can sometimes be overshadowed by limiting beliefs, often rooted in societal stereotypes or personal experiences of exclusion.

These beliefs "limit" our thinking of how much success we're capable of achieving and how much money we "deserve" to earn. When we're stuck in limiting beliefs, we put an invisible cap on our potential and unconsciously tell ourselves that nothing can change. When you believe this thinking, you end up settling in your life, whether it's where you want to be or not.

Reflection: *Take a few minutes to reflect right now about your personal limiting beliefs or fears about money. What does that look like? What do you tell yourself subconsciously that prevents you from making changes?*

Self-doubt, low self-esteem, or imposter syndrome all play a part in the vicious cycle of limiting beliefs. Some limiting beliefs and/or fears surrounding your business might look like:

- "I can't charge that much!"

- "There's no way my business could ever bring in that much money per month."
- "I don't understand how other entrepreneurs make so much money."
- "I'm not an expert or authority."
- "No one cares what I have to say."
- "No one would pay me that much."
- "There's no point in me doing [this-or-that]– somebody else has already done it and done it better."

Does any of this sound familiar? If you can relate to any of the above, don't sweat it. The first step is acknowledging it. The next step is rewiring these beliefs and elevating your CEO mindset to allow you and your business to soar.

Growth Mindset

Developing a growth mindset is essential as it fosters resilience, innovation, and a willingness to take calculated risks. To cultivate a growth mindset, it is crucial to start by analyzing and reframing your beliefs about success and failure. Embracing challenges and viewing them as opportunities for growth is a fundamental shift in perspective. By reframing failure as a steppingstone to success, one can overcome the fear of failure and maintain a positive attitude towards setbacks.

Advantages of Growth Mindset

When you have a growth mindset, you understand that you have the power to change your life. You learn from past mistakes, and you look forward to the future. You may not fully understand HOW to make life-altering changes yet, but you believe you can figure it out by asking questions and doing research. A growth mindset sparks excitement about what's possible and that excitement spurs action to make your dreams and goals a reality.

Play #2: Develop Your Business Idea

We can achieve what we can conceive and believe.
– Mark Twain

Entrepreneurs are often celebrated as the backbone of the nation. With passion and drive, anyone can become a successful entrepreneur, provided the planning and execution are done well. The first step to embarking on an entrepreneurial journey is choosing the ideal business, which will be determined by its feasibility as well as your own interests and expertise.

Identifying a Problem or Need

In the entrepreneurship world, success is built upon identifying and solving problems or unmet needs. You must possess a keen eye for spotting opportunities.

Market Research and Analysis

A successful venture requires a deep understanding of the market and the competition. You need to discover if the market is profitable and how you can carve out a competitive edge. Understanding the market and its impact on your business equips you to face upcoming challenges and enhances your chances of success.

Is It Feasible?

You may be passionate about an idea, but if it isn't feasible, it's unlikely to succeed. Feasibility pertains to how simple or complex it is to execute an idea, influenced by various factors. For instance, a dog bakery might thrive in a city with many dog lovers but struggle in one with fewer. Before advancing with any idea, its feasibility must be assessed. This involves understanding the market and your potential customers, topics we'll delve into more deeply in later sections. To evaluate feasibility, consider the following questions:

- Do you have the necessary funding?
- Is there a market for your product?
- What is the market's outlook?
- Can you price your product competitively?
- How will you operate?
- Will you have a sufficient customer base for long-term success?

What Are Your Interests?

Entrepreneurship is challenging. If you don't enjoy what you do, success is unlikely. Before selecting your business, consider your hobbies and interests and explore how to turn them into profitable ventures. For example, a love for animals might lead to a pet-sitting service, while a passion for cooking could inspire a food truck business.

Do You Have the Experience?

Experience and expertise significantly benefit any business. Understanding the difference between the two can help you identify your own strengths. Experience is gained through observation, encounters, and actions, and many jobs provide it. For instance, working as a server offers experience in the restaurant industry but doesn't necessarily equate to expertise. Utilize your experiences to help choose your business direction. Years in customer service, for example, would be beneficial for a customer-oriented business.

Are You an Expert?

Expertise encompasses knowledge and skills acquired through education and training, often from work in specialized positions or degrees in specific fields. An accountant or chef, for example, would be considered experts in their respective fields. Expertise enhances your capability to run a business effectively. If you haven't reached expert status yet, don't give up on your idea. Passion can propel you toward becoming an expert through classes or internships. Another option is to partner with someone who already possesses expertise.

Is the Venture Lucrative?

Before embarking on any venture, determine if it is lucrative. This requires understanding the niche market you're interested in. Some business trends are apparent, while others are not. Tools like Google Trends can help you gauge how the market is evolving and whether your interest remains profitable.

Is There Competition?

Most new ventures face competition. It's rare to come across truly original ideas; many are adaptations of existing markets (e.g. video streaming over rental stores). Once familiar with your market, your first task is to identify your competition, focusing on those closest to your product or service. For example, a coffee shop is not the main competitor of a restaurant. Understanding their strengths and weaknesses can give you a competitive advantage. Pay close attention to their objectives to identify potential weaknesses you can exploit.

How Can You Set Yourself Apart from the Competition?

By understanding your competition, you can distinguish your business. You've already pinpointed where your competition is lacking; now, you can fill that niche. For instance, emphasizing customer service can attract customers who are willing to pay more for it. Other ways to stand out include:

- **Expertise:** Utilize your knowledge to attract customers.

- **Value:** Demonstrate how you offer better value than your competitors.

- **Communication:** Find creative and innovative ways to connect with customers.

How Is the Customer Prospect?

You cannot create a successful venture without fully understanding your customers. Success hinges on identifying what customers want and providing it. Start by understanding the demographics in your area for insights into spending habits and values. Panels and surveys can offer deeper customer insights. Continued feedback allows you to tailor your business to meet customer needs continuously.

Play #3: Find Your Niche

I know the price of success: dedication, hard work and an unremitting devotion to the things you want to see happen. – Frank Lloyd Wright

One of my most significant challenges in entrepreneurship was my desire to help everybody. I eventually realized that not everyone was my ideal customer.

While you may have a desire to help everyone, the secret to standout success is not about being everything to everyone but about being everything to someone. Mastering the art and science of identifying your target market is essential. You have to get stalker specific (in a non-creepy way) about who you want to serve.

Consider the process of discovering your niche or target audience as embarking on a treasure hunt. You wouldn't start searching for hidden treasure without a map, right? Similarly, diving into business without understanding your niche is similar to setting sail without a compass. You might end up lost at sea or in a sea of sameness, making it difficult to distinguish yourself from your competitors.

Why Choose a Niche?

Spotlight Effect: In a niche, your business can shine like a lighthouse beacon. It's easier to become a big fish in a small pond than a minnow in the ocean.

Laser-Sharp Marketing: Knowing your niche allows you to tailor your marketing messages so precisely that your audience feels like you're reading their minds.

Fewer Competitors: The more specific your niche, the fewer competitors you'll have. It's like being in a league of your own, where you set the rules and standards.

The Niche Navigator

After pinpointing your unique niche, it's time to position yourself as the go-to expert. Here's a guide to mastering your chosen field:

Speak Their Language: Use the words and phrases your niche audience uses. It builds trust and establishes you as one of them.

Be Where They Are: If your niche hangs out on Instagram, you should be there too. Tailor your online presence to the platforms your audience prefers.

Offer Tailored Solutions: Your products or services

should feel custom-made for your niche. It's the difference between a bespoke suit and a one-size-fits-all jumpsuit.

Mastering your niche is about finding your tribe, understanding their needs, and serving them passionately. It's the cornerstone of branding, marketing, and product development. So, embark on your niche expedition with curiosity, and remember, the riches are in the niches!

Play #4: Lay the Foundation: Business Basics

Embarking on the journey to start your own business can be exciting, scary, and a bit intimidating. It requires detailed planning and courageous actions at every step.

These actions include choosing a name, structure, and location for the business. Equally important is registering your business and securing an accountant to assist with financial matters. All these steps lay the groundwork for launching a successful business.

Decide on a Name

Choosing a name is more challenging than it appears. You want the name to stand out and reflect your brand's image. Names too similar to those of competitors can lead to legal issues and fail to distinguish your business. If you find it difficult to come up with a name, consider seeking assistance from a naming firm or using artificial intelligence (AI) tools like ChatGPT to get started.

Tips for Choosing a Name:

- Consider clever wordplay but avoid corny puns.

- Keep it simple; your name should be clear without needing explanation.

- Ensure your name works as a website domain; it should be short and easy to remember.

Good Example:
BakeItEasy.com. This name is short, memorable, and clearly indicates a business related to baking, making it perfect for a bakery or baking tools company.

Bad Example:
TheIncredibleEmporiumOfBakedGoodsAndConfections.com

Whew! That's quite a mouthful. Despite being descriptive, this domain name is too long, hard to remember, and prone to typos, making it less than ideal for an online presence.

GoDaddy, Namecheap, and Google Domains are popular platforms where you can check the availability of your desired business name. If your first choice is taken, these services often suggest variations, helping you find a close match that is still available for registration.

By following these tips, you can select a business name that is not only catchy and effective but also well-suited for your online branding efforts.

Business Legal Structure

Before taking any action, it's crucial to determine the legal structure of your business. There are various legal structures suitable for any type of company you wish to start, each offering its own set of advantages and disadvantages. To select the appropriate structure, having a clear understanding of your expectations and goals for your business is important.

Types of business:

- **Sole proprietorship** – The simplest business to create, it also carries the greatest financial risk due to unlimited personal liability.
- **General partnership** – A business run by two or more individuals where all partners are equally responsible for the actions of one, if made in the name of the business.
- **Limited Partnership** – Decision-making power is limited to specific individuals, as outlined in the business agreement.
- **C Corporation** – Corporations are taxed separately from the owners, facing taxation on both corporate earnings and shareholder dividends.
- **S Corporation** – Profits are passed through to the owners' personal tax returns via an IRS tax election, avoiding double taxation.

- **LLC (Limited Liability Company):** Combines the characteristics of partnerships and sole proprietorships with the tax benefits of S Corporations.

Register the Business

Once you've chosen a name and structure, you need to register your business and obtain the necessary licenses, permits, and identification. This process varies by state and business type.

- **EIN:** Except for sole proprietors without employees, you'll likely need an Employer Identification Number (EIN) from the IRS.

- **DBA:** A "Doing Business As" (DBA) is typically filed at the county clerk's office when the company operates under a name different from the owner's. Requirements vary by state.

- **Business Licenses and Permits:** Licensing is mandated at the federal and state levels, depending on the business. Federal licensing is necessary for businesses involved in alcohol, agriculture, transportation, etc. Always verify with federal, state, and local guidelines to ensure compliance with all licensing and permit requirements.

Choose the Location

Unless your business is entirely remote or online, choosing the right location is crucial. Begin by checking for any zoning restrictions. Then, evaluate safety and affordability. A safe location not only attracts customers but also creates a desirable workplace for employees.

Other Considerations:

- **Image:** Select a location that aligns with your business image (edgy, artsy, upscale, etc.).

- **Competition:** Opt for a location where you complement, rather than compete with, neighboring businesses.

- **Growth:** If expansion is in your plans, ensure the location offers room for growth.

Hire an Accountant

Securing a trustworthy accountant from the start is advisable. Look for someone who offers more than tax preparation; you want a business advisor. Consider the following when choosing an accountant:

- Experience with your type of business
- Industry expertise
- Range of services offered

- Direct communication availability
- Compatibility with your business needs and comfort in the working relationship

Do not engage with anyone who lacks the necessary services or with whom you feel uncomfortable establishing a business relationship.

Play #5: Create a Business Plan

A goal without a plan is just a wish.- Antoine de Saint Exupery

A strong business plan is necessary for long-term growth and success. It functions as a roadmap, delineating the objectives, strategies, and operations of a company. Additionally, it serves as a tool to attract investors, secure funding, and establish credibility. Planning requires the collection of pertinent information and the drafting of the plan, incorporating all the essential elements. Although the creation of a business plan might appear tedious, it should not be neglected.

What Should Be Included in the Business Plan?

The business plan must include several basic elements, such as:

- **Executive summary** – Provides an overview of the company and includes information from other sections. This is typically written last because the introduction is so important.
- **Market analysis** – Provides information about the market, including industry and pricing.

- **Company description** – Provides information about the nature of the business and the factors that will make it successful.
- **Management and organization** – Offers a view of the company's structure, leadership, and team.
- **Sales and marketing** – Provides information about the sales strategies and marketing approaches that will be used.
- **Product/service** – Explains the value, benefits, and uniqueness of the product or service.
- **Funding/financial** – Outlines the amount of money the company needs in different scenarios and creates a five-year financial plan.

Gather Documentation

Before starting a business plan, it is necessary to gather the required documentation. This information will guide the business plan.

Documentation to Gather:

- **Vision statement**: Establishes the company's value and purpose.
- **Mission statement**: Explains the company's value, interest, and goals, including

statements of purpose, strategy, value, standards, and benefits.

- **SWOT analysis**: Outlines the strengths, weaknesses, opportunities, and threats the business faces.
- **Financial documentation**: Includes all financial documents and projections related to the startup.

Develop a Business Plan Outline

Once all the documentation is gathered, use it to create the outline. Like any other important document, the business plan should have an outline before it is written. The elements can guide the outline.

Elements that should be in outlines:

- **Coversheet** – Includes the name, address, and title
- **Table of contents**
- **Executive summary** – Overview, mission statement, opportunity, requirements, competitors, advantages, etc.
- **Market analysis** – Target market, trends, research, strategy.
- **Company description** – Mission, business model, SWOT, strategic relationships, and strategy.

- **Organization management** – Structure, location, personnel, security, insurance, accounting.
- **Sales and marketing** – Method of sales, pricing, branding, networking, strategies, incentives.
- **Product/service** – Product definition and any plans for expansion.
- **Funding/financial** – Financial needs, cash flow, dispersal, three-year projection, balance sheet, break even analysis, financial history, analysis.
- **Supporting documents** – Includes resumes, financial statements, credit report, references, legal documents, other documents.

Draft a Business Plan

Once the outline is created, begin drafting the business plan. Drafting the entire plan can be overwhelming, but remember these tips to help create an effective business plan:

- Work on the elements of the plan individually.
- Focus on your niche and what makes your plan stand out.
- Use clear and concise language.
- End with the executive summary.
- Rewrite the draft frequently.

Play #6: Secure the Funding

"The highest use of capital is not to make more money, but to make money do more for the betterment of life." – Henry Ford

One of the most significant challenges entrepreneurs face is the lack of funding. Starting a business requires capital, and securing the necessary funds can be a grueling task. Entrepreneurs must be resourceful in finding investors, leveraging personal savings, or exploring alternative financing options such as crowdfunding or business loans. Building a solid business plan and showcasing the potential growth can greatly increase the chances of securing funding.

There are numerous financing options and resources available for entrepreneurs starting their funding search. Consulting with those who have previously navigated this path can offer invaluable insights. The next step is to explore all your options.

Contact Organizations for Guidance

The more informed you are, the better equipped you will be to make the right decisions on financing for your business. Via mentors and informational websites, there are many organizations dedicated to helping new businesses. Contacting one or more of these organizations and discussing with people who understand what your needs are is a crucial step as it provides some great information.

The Service Corps of Retired Executives (SCORE) association is a nonprofit organization that is dedicated to helping businesses. They have retired and volunteer executives on staff to mentor entrepreneurs. They also provide workshops, seminars, and a wealth of information on their website. While some of their services may cost a little money, many of their services are free to use. Here are some websites and associations to go to for help:

- **The U.S. Small Business Administration** - *Offers tips on financing your business with government assistance*- sba.gov
- **Business USA** - *Offers lots of information and resources for a business*-business.usa.gov
- **SCORE** -*Offers tons of information, mentoring, & resources*- score.org
- **Entrepreneur** - *Offers advice, information, and some services. They also have a magazine publication*-entrepreneur.com

AN ENTREPRENEUR'S PLAYBOOK

Decide the Type of Financing

Now that you have resources to inform you about your financing options, it's time to decide which type of financing you are looking for. It is imperative that you take the time to consider your options carefully. Choosing an unsuitable option could jeopardize your business's future before it has the opportunity to thrive. Here are a few of the different types of financing options:

- **Self-financing** – Self-financing means that you provide the funds needed to start the business. According to *Entrepreneur* magazine, it is the number one source of start-up financing for small businesses. You can save up money, use preexisting savings, borrow against your 401(k), use the funds in your IRA, borrow against your life insurance, or take out a home equity loan.
- **Grants-** There are many different types of grants available. Some grants are state and regional, some are based on minority or veteran status, and others depend on the type of business you are trying to start. Although there is significant competition for grants, they are an excellent option because you do not have to pay them back!
- **Financing from friends or family members-** Friends or family members who have extra money and want to help see your business vision

come to life are a great resource for financing. The downside to using financing from family and friends is you have to be very clear about when their investment can be returned to them.

- **Financing from bank loans** - Bank loans are a great option for financing. Bank loans are based on your credit, a solid business plan, experience, assets, and a personal guarantee that the loan will be paid back. If you are taking the bank loan route, be sure to contact different banks, and get the best interest rate.

- **Small Business Administration (SBA) Loans-** The Small Business Administration (SBA) offers several types of loans designed to meet the needs of small businesses, including minority-owned businesses. These loans are particularly beneficial because they often come with lower interest rates and longer repayment terms compared to those available from traditional lenders, making them an attractive option for entrepreneurs. For minority-owned businesses, the SBA also provides specific programs and resources aimed at leveling the playing field and improving access to funding and business support services.

- **Financing from investors-** The three most common types of investors are private equity, venture capital, and angel investing. Private equity investors are typically individuals or privately owned companies. Venture capital investors, while also a form of private equity, tend to be more hands-on. They often bring managerial or technical expertise to the table to help grow the business. Lastly, angel investing involves individuals who invest in businesses that may not attract the attention of venture capitalists. These investors usually receive stock or equity in the company.

- **Crowdfunding**- Crowdfunding is a platform where entrepreneurs create a compelling pitch and leverage their network or even attract strangers to invest in their business idea.

Shop Around

You wouldn't go to a car lot and buy the first car you see, would you? Not likely. You want to shop around and see what is available to you. Just like in any major purchase, or financial commitment, you want to explore your options. Starting a business is a major life and financial event. Rushing into the first financing option available is not advisable. Talk to as many business owners as possible to discover their financing sources. Go to multiple banks, if you are looking for a loan, and try to get the best rates. Contact your government agencies and explore what grants you are qualified for. Shop around for the best prices on equipment and buildings. Shopping around doesn't cost you money, but failing to do so might. We've all experienced buyer's remorse—like buying a pair of shoes only to find them cheaper elsewhere. It leaves you feeling disappointed for having overpaid. Do yourself a favor and don't make that mistake with such a large financial commitment, look around and make sure the grass isn't greener somewhere else!

Play #7: Build a Team

I'm reminded of an African Proverb: *"If you want to go fast, go alone; if you want to go far, go together."*

This proverb emphasizes the value of teamwork and collaboration over individual effort when it comes to achieving long-term or significant goals. It highlights the importance of community and collective effort in reaching greater distances or achieving more substantial outcomes than one might alone.

In the grand game of entrepreneurship, mastering the art of delegation is like unlocking a new level of strategic play. Many small business owners inadvertently cap their potential for growth by wearing too many hats. They juggle sales, service, marketing, taxes, and the myriad other tasks that come with running a business. This relentless multitasking doesn't lead to a badge of honor; instead, it often results in stress, burnout, and frustratingly stagnant growth. The truth is, there's a limit to how much one person can do—and how far one person can go—alone.

Many small business owners stay small because they never realize this. However, when that "aha" moment strikes, and you realize you can do more, and grow faster, when you get help, then you start to see exponential growth!

It's a pivotal shift, moving from solo player to team captain. The transition might feel unnerving at first. It requires trust—trust in others to handle aspects of your vision with the same care and dedication you would. It also demands a shift in mindset, from valuing individual productivity to valuing collaborative synergy.

Understanding the Importance of Teamwork

Building a team is not just about filling roles; it's about creating a collective force where the sum is greater than its parts. It's about finding people who not only have the skills but also share your passion and vision. When you start to build your team, consider not just what your business does, but why it does it. Aligning your team around a shared purpose is the key to unlocking true potential.

Building the Right Team

As you embark on this journey, remember that building a team is both a challenge and an opportunity. When it comes to building a diverse team, it is crucial to prioritize skills, experience, and cultural fit. The right team can propel your business to heights you never imagined, turning obstacles into stepping stones for innovation and growth. So, take the leap, start building your dream team, and watch as your business transforms from a solo endeavor to a symphony of collaborative success. This is your playbook's power play for building a team that not only shares your workload but multiplies your success.

Recruitment

To reach potential candidates effectively, utilize multiple recruitment channels. Posting job opening on online job boards, leveraging social media platforms, and networking within your industry are all effective methods. Other sites such as Fiverr, Freelancer.com, and Upwork might be options if you're interested in freelance services.

Play #8: Systemize and Automate Your Business

"We are what we repeatedly do. Excellence, therefore, is not an act but a habit. – Aristotle

If you want to control costs while allowing for significant growth, you need to have systems in place and use technology to automate your business. Incorporating these processes will help with streamlining business operations allowing you to work less, earn more, and scale your business—without burning out!

Here are some strategies:

Standard Operating Procedures (SOP) manual - An SOP manual is a comprehensive document providing step-by-step instructions for completing tasks or procedures. This is a great resource for quickly and efficiently training new employees.

Schedule and Delegate Content Creation – Successful businesses recognize the importance of regular engagement with clients, customers, and potential customers. Consistently producing content can be overwhelming and time consuming. The solution—schedule and delegate all content creation.

Automate Content Promotion – Advancements in technology and online tools have simplified the automation of content and business promotion. Most social media tools allow you to schedule your post ahead of time, so you don't have to worry about posting content if you're on vacation or sick. Another plus is that most social media automation software also analyzes the performance of posts across your social media platforms. This helps you see what your readers most respond to, when they prefer seeing your posts, and which sites reach more people i.e. Facebook, Instagram, TikTok.

Utilize electronic payment processing- Make it easy for customers to give you money. Requiring them to mail a check or money order might lead them to reconsider their purchase. Services like Stripe or PayPal allow for immediate payment acceptance.

Setup Email Autoresponders- Email autoresponder software, such as AWeber, Mailchimp, and Constant Contact, can automate communication with your customers.

Automate appointment scheduling- Platforms like Calendly, TidyCal, and Acuity Scheduling automate the appointment booking process. These tools not only provide a hassle-free way for customers to schedule appointments based on real-time availability but also integrate with your digital ecosystem, sending reminders and facilitating appointment rescheduling with ease.

Utilizing Customer Relationship Management (CRM) Systems in Business

In the digital age, leveraging technology to streamline operations and enhance customer relationships is not just an option; it's a necessity for business success. Automated systems, especially Customer Relationship Management (CRM) tools, stand at the forefront of this transformation. These systems are the linchpins in understanding customer needs, enhancing communication, and driving sales. These platforms can be key in your entrepreneurial strategy.

CRM systems have evolved from simple contact management solutions to comprehensive platforms that manage sales, marketing, customer service, and more. They offer a unified repository for customer data, which can significantly improve customer service and sales efforts. By automating routine tasks, CRMs allow businesses to focus on strategy and growth, making them indispensable in today's fast-paced market environment.

Noteworthy CRM Systems

There are many CRM systems on the market at various price points. You can research which software best meets your needs. The following are some examples of CRM systems that cater to a variety of business needs:

Groove.cm (previously known as Groove Funnels): A CRM and business management platform. It's designed to support entrepreneurs in creating, managing, and growing their online presence with ease. Beyond traditional CRM functionalities, Groove.cm offers tools for website and funnel building, email marketing, online sales, and much more. Its integrated approach means you can manage nearly all aspects of your business from one place, enhancing efficiency and reducing the need for multiple software solutions.

Systeme.io: An all-in-one online business platform designed to provide entrepreneurs and small to medium-sized businesses with the tools they need to launch, grow, and scale their online operations. It's known for its affordability and ease of use, making it an attractive choice for those new to online business or with limited technical skills.

HubSpot: Known for its inbound marketing emphasis, HubSpot offers a free CRM that integrates seamlessly with its marketing, sales, and service hubs.

Zoho CRM: An option for small to medium-sized businesses, Zoho CRM provides a good balance of features at an affordable price. Offers a wide range of business applications and tools for sales and marketing automation, as well as productivity and collaboration.

Keap (formerly Infusionsoft) - Best known for its advanced automation and customer relationship management tools for small businesses, combining CRM, marketing automation, and e-commerce functionalities.

InfluencerSoft: A marketing automation platform designed to cater specifically to entrepreneurs, coaches, influencers, and small to medium-sized businesses. The platform is aimed at helping users efficiently manage and automate their sales funnels, marketing campaigns, and online courses, among other features.

Maximizing the Potential of Automated Systems

To fully leverage the power of automated systems and CRM platforms, consider these strategies:

Integration: Ensure your CRM system integrates seamlessly with other tools and platforms your business uses. This creates a cohesive ecosystem that enhances efficiency and data accuracy.

Customization: Tailor your CRM to fit your business processes. Custom fields, workflows, and reports can align the system with your specific operational needs.

Training: Invest in training for your team to maximize the system's effectiveness. Familiarity with the CRM's features can lead to innovative uses that drive business growth.

Data Analysis: Use the data and analytics provided by your CRM to make informed decisions. Understanding customer behaviors and preferences can guide your marketing and product development efforts.

Incorporating automated systems and CRM platforms into your business strategy is not just about keeping up with technology—it's about setting your business up for scalable growth and deeper customer connections. By choosing the right platform, you're equipping your business with the resources it needs to thrive in the competitive digital landscape. Remember, the goal is to work smarter, not harder, and automated systems are key players in making that a reality.

Play #9: Market the Business

The aim of marketing is to know and understand the customer so well the product or service fits him and sells itself. – Peter F. Drucker

Marketing is essential to the success of any business. Marketing is the art of grabbing the potential customer's attention. Your business cannot afford to be hidden, as though it were in some sort of covert witness protection program. In other words, it can't be the best-kept secret that nobody knows about. You must broadcast the existence of your business far and wide. Marketing isn't just a part of the business; it's a necessity. Being invisible doesn't attract customers! The way you market your business varies depending on your product. Let's explore some marketing options.

Implementing Digital Marketing Strategies

The first step in implementing digital marketing strategies is to define clear goals and objectives. Whether it's increasing website traffic, improving conversion rates, or expanding online presence, having clear goals will provide a clear direction for your marketing campaign.

As mentioned earlier in the chapter on finding your

niche, recognizing your target audience and creating buyer personas is essential. Getting to know the demographics, interests, and behaviors of your target audience allows you to customize your marketing messages and select the most effective channels to reach them. Refer to the persona example of **Fitness- Focused Fiona** for insight.

Persona Name: Fitness-Focused Fiona

Age: 29

Occupation: Marketing Manager

Location: Urban city, living in an apartment.

Education: Bachelor's degree in Communications

Income: $65,000 per year

Marital Status: Single

Children: None

Social Media Use: Active on Instagram and YouTube, uses these platforms for fitness inspiration, tips, and to stay connected with fitness communities.

Goals:

- To maintain a healthy lifestyle while balancing a busy work schedule.

- To find quick, effective workouts that can be done at home or in a small gym.
- To improve her strength and stamina without spending hours in the gym.

Challenges:

- Struggles to find time for long workouts due to her demanding job.
- Feels overwhelmed by the abundance of fitness information online.
- Has limited space for workouts in her apartment.

What She Values:

- Efficiency and flexibility in workout routines.
- A supportive community that motivates her to stay on track.
- Clear, straightforward fitness guidance without gimmicks.

Buying Motivation:

- Wants a program that fits into her busy schedule and doesn't require a lot of equipment.
- Looks for testimonials from other professionals who have succeeded with the program.
- Prefers a subscription with a trial period to test the program before committing financially.

Buying Concerns:

- Worried about the cost of the program and if it will fit into her budget.
- Concerned that she might lose motivation without in-person classes.
- Unsure if the program can be personalized to her fitness level and goals.

Additionally, the following types of businesses could see Fiona as an ideal customer:

Online Fitness Platforms: Subscription-based services offering virtual classes or personalized workout plans that can be done at home or on-the-go, catering to her need for efficiency and flexibility.

Fitness Apparel and Equipment Companies: Brands specializing in home workout gear, such as yoga mats, resistance bands, or compact exercise equipment that fits her living space and lifestyle.

Health and Wellness Apps: Mobile applications that track fitness progress, provide nutrition advice, or offer short, effective workout routines could appeal to her desire for straightforward fitness guidance.

Meal Kit and Healthy Food Delivery Services: Companies that deliver healthy, easy-to-prepare meals or snacks that align with her nutritional goals and busy lifestyle.

Fitness Influencers and Bloggers: Content creators who focus on health, wellness, and fitness tips for busy professionals can connect with Fiona through social media or their blogs, offering inspiration and community.

Community Fitness Events: Local or virtual 5K runs, charity fitness challenges, or group workout events that provide a sense of community and motivation to stay active.

Create a Website

In today's world, almost everyone uses smartphones, tablets, or computers to browse the internet. Statistics from the 2023-2024 United States Census show that 94% of households own a computer, and 88.3% have internet access. Given this widespread use of the internet as a marketing tool, the absence of a website for your business can be seen as a significant missed opportunity.

Creating a website is an easy way to get your company out to the public. There are lots of places online that provide web hosting for under $100 a year. You will want to do some research to decide which company you want to host your site with. Once that is complete, the next step is designing your site. Creating a webpage that is functional is a big factor in setting up your website. You will want to make sure that it is easy for the consumer to use and navigate. The website needs to look clean and professional, and when people visit it, they should understand instantly what your product or service is.

What should your website have?

- **An about us page**- Give the public some insight on your company, what your values and beliefs are, and how you got started.

- **Contact us page**- Here is a place you can provide your company address, phone number, emails, or a contact form for customers to leave their information for follow-up.
- **A product/ services page**- Use this page to describe your product or services offered, and it could be the storefront for customers to make direct purchases.
- **FAQ**- Answer frequently asked questions that you get about your products or services in this area.

Ensuring your website contains these elements can significantly enhance the visitor experience, making it easier for potential customers to learn about and engage with your business.

Social Media

More than half the population has a presence on social media platforms such as Facebook, Instagram, TikTok, Pinterest, or Twitter. Consumers utilize these platforms to stay connected with friends, while savvy businesses have learned to leverage these sites to keep their customers engaged with their products. Past WebDAM data reported that 52% of all marketers have found a customer via Facebook. They also found that emails including social media buttons have a click-through rate 158% higher than those without social media buttons. Consider the expansive reach your company could achieve by establishing a social media presence.

These platforms can serve as venues for posting discount codes, company news, or just entertaining facts. Advertising aims to convey the product and the company's name/image to the consumer, and social media offers an excellent channel for this purpose! Establishing Facebook, Instagram, TikTok, Pinterest, or Twitter accounts are essentially cost-free. While additional advertising on these sites comes at a cost, building a substantial fan base can suffice for all your social media advertising needs. Given the accessibility and cost-effectiveness of social media, why wouldn't you seize this opportunity?

Use the Power of Networking

Networking involves exchanging information or services with people, groups, or organizations to build productive relationships for employment or business.

Networking groups provide numerous benefits, acting as valuable resources for product enhancement, marketing support, and expert advice. Comprised of individuals with shared interests, such as business ownership, these groups facilitate the exchange of insights, discussions on marketing strategies, and the opportunity to purchase products.

Beyond bolstering your confidence in business, networking groups provide connections and opportunities that might otherwise be inaccessible. Participating in these groups can be both enjoyable and beneficial, functioning as a sort of "business social club." Within these circles, you can foster relationships with like-minded individuals, consequently boosting both your personal and your company's reputation.

Play #10: Provide Exceptional Customer Service

You can design and create, and build the most wonderful place in the world. But it takes people to make the dream a reality. - Walt Disney

The way you treat a customer has everything to do with building the know, like and trust factor causing the customer to come back, again and again.

Scenario 1: One of my vehicles is the "Ultimate Driving Machine". When I walk in the door of the dealership for service, I'm greeted and assigned a personal service advisor who keeps me updated on the status of my vehicle during the process. I receive a text with link to a recorded video from the service technician explaining what they're doing and any other issues they've found. There is a free snack area, big screen TVs, Wi-Fi, workstations, and Starbuck-like coffee center while you wait. At one dealership, there is even a movie theater where you can hang out while your car is being serviced. I can also call in advance to arrange for a loaner vehicle if I need to drop my car off and not wait. Even though I sometimes pay a higher price for service, I take my car to the dealer because I like how I'm treated, and

I trust them to fix my issue and offer a warranty if my issue is not resolved.

Scenario 2: I had some damage to the roof of one of my residences due to a windstorm. Every time the wind blew afterward, there were shingles flapping and blowing everywhere, which eventually led to leaks. I called several so-called reputable roofing companies to give me quotes, and many failed to show up to give me an estimate. I called a small, family-owned roofing and remodeling company, which promptly gave me an estimate. Noticing the severity of the damage and being aware of impending bad weather expected to arrive that week, using his own materials, he climbed up on the roof and installed a covering to help shield the roof until it could be fixed. This kind gesture resonated volumes with me. I gave him the job and used him for another job. I also hired an electrician that he referred.

In today's competitive environment, providing an exceptional customer experience is crucial for fostering loyalty. Businesses should strive to deliver on their promises, exceed customer expectations by offering personalized services, responding promptly to inquiries and complaints, and continuously improving products or services based on customer feedback.

By prioritizing customer satisfaction, entrepreneurs

can foster strong relationships, build brand loyalty, and gain a competitive edge.

In today's digital age, word-of-mouth travels fast, and customers have the power to influence your brand's reputation though online reviews and social media. By consistently providing exceptional customer service, going the extra mile to exceed expectations, you can create a positive impression and generate brand advocates who will champion your business.

Conclusion

In conclusion, starting your own business offers a multitude of benefits—from pursuing your passion and achieving financial independence to enjoying flexibility and personal growth, and from making a meaningful impact to establishing a lasting legacy. If you are an aspiring entrepreneur, seize the opportunities that await you. The secret to entrepreneurial success does not lie in a single element, but in a combination of factors working together. Keep in mind that as you build your empire, it is ok to start small and evolve. The journey may present challenges, but the rewards are undoubtedly worth it.

My Social Media Hangouts:

Facebook:
https://www.facebook.com/biztalkwithora/

Instagram:
https://www.instagram.com/biztalkwithora/

YouTube:
https://www.yo
utube.com/watch?v=UPbRAEW8tfw&t=1281s

Book Website: www.anentrepreneursplaybook.com

Note: Visit the website for a free download of more tools, templates and resources to accompany this book at www.anentrepreneursplaybook.com.

About the Author

Ora M. Chisom, MBA, PMP, is the dynamic force behind "An Entrepreneur's Playbook: 10 Power Plays for Business Success." A seasoned business strategist and technology enthusiast, Ora has made it her life's work to empower aspiring entrepreneurs with the knowledge and tools they need to build diverse income streams and achieve financial independence.

Ora's commitment to education and empowerment extends beyond the pages of her book. She has invested years in teaching workforce development and career advancement skills, helping countless individuals elevate their careers to new heights.

Drawing from years of experience, Ora distills her expertise into this essential guide for both seasoned professionals and budding business owners. Her multifaceted approach as an entrepreneur, speaker, author, and podcast host allows her to reach and inspire a wide audience, sharing her conviction that with the right resources, anyone can launch and nurture a successful enterprise.